Bilingual Edition

Let's Draw with Shapes™

Edición Bilingüe

Let's Draw a Frog with Ovals

Vamos a dibujar una rana usando óvalos

Kathy Kuhtz Campbell
Illustrations by Emily Muschinske

Traducción al español:
María Cristina Brusca

The Rosen Publishing Group's
PowerStart Press™ & **Editorial Buenas Letras**™
New York

Published in 2004 by The Rosen Publishing Group, Inc.
29 East 21st Street, New York, NY 10010

First Edition

Book Design: Emily Muschinske

Photo Credits: Photograph of frog on pp. 23, 24 © Michael & Patricia Fogden/CORBIS.

Campbell, Kathy Kuhtz
Let's draw a frog with ovals = Vamos a dibujar una rana usando óvalos / Kathy Kuhtz Campbell ; illustrations by Emily Muschinske ; translated by María Cristina Brusca.
p. cm. — (Let's draw with shapes)
Includes index.
Summary: This book offers simple instructions for using ovals to draw a frog.
ISBN 1-4042-7503-7 (lib.)
1. Frogs in art—Juvenile literature 2. Ovals—Juvenile literature 3. Drawing—Technique—Juvenile literature
[1. Frogs in art 2. Drawing—Technique 3. Spanish language materials—Bilingual]
I. Muschinske, Emily, ill. II. Title. III.Series.
NC655 .C363 2004   2003009129
743.6'789—dc21

Manufactured in the United States of America

Due to the changing nature of Internet links, PowerStart Press has developed an online list of Web sites related to the subject of this book. This site is updated regularly. Please use this link to access the list:

http://www.buenasletraslinks.com/ldwsh/rana

2

Contents

Contenido

Draw a large yellow oval
for the body of your frog.

Dibuja un óvalo grande,
amarillo, para hacer
el cuerpo de tu rana.

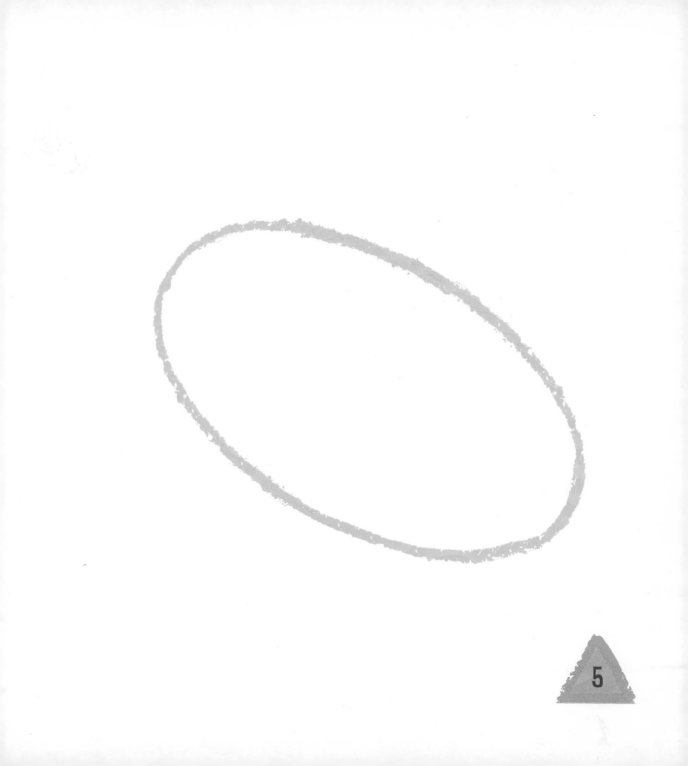

5

Draw two small orange ovals for the front leg of your frog.

Dibuja dos pequeños óvalos anaranjados para la pata delantera de tu rana.

6

7

Draw two red ovals for the back leg of your frog.

___

Dibuja dos óvalos rojos para la pata trasera de tu rana.

9

Add two green ovals for the front and back feet of your frog.

Agrega dos óvalos verdes para los pies delanteros y traseros de tu rana.

Draw a small blue oval for one of the eyes of your frog.

Dibuja un pequeño óvalo azul para hacer uno de los ojos de tu rana.

Add a purple oval for the other eye of your frog.

Agrega un óvalo violeta para hacer el segundo ojo de tu rana.

14

Draw a pink oval for the mouth of your frog.

Dibuja un óvalo rosa para la boca de tu rana.

16

Add a black oval for the head and two small black ovals on top.

Dibuja un óvalo negro para la cabeza. Agrégale arriba dos pequeños óvalos negros.

Color in your frog.

Colorea tu rana.

This frog can go up a tree.

Esta rana puede subir
a un árbol.

23

Words to Know
Palabras que debes saber

body
cuerpo

feet
pies

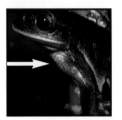

front
delantero

mouth
boca

Colors
Colores

red / rojo

orange / anaranjado

yellow / amarillo

green / verde

blue / azul

purple / violeta

pink / rosa

black / negro

Index

Índice

24